I0177812

D. DOUG GIBSON

GOOD — AS — NEW

A CHILD'S GUIDE TO BECOMING A CHRISTIAN

STUDENT WORKBOOK

college
press
Joplin, Missouri

**college
press**

Good as New: A Child's Guide to Becoming a Christian
Copyright © 2000 College Press Publishing

Updated cover and text design in 2024.

All rights reserved.

ISBN: 9780899008349 (paperback)
ISBN: 9780899008400 (ePub)

Art Direction: Chad Harrington (YouPublish.com)
Cover Design: Nate Farro (YouPublish.com)

CONTENTS

Dear Parents,

For some time now you have been faithfully bringing your children up in the ways of the Lord. You have been bringing them with you to church, giving them a chance to learn about our Savior and to worship Him. I commend you! You could not be doing anything more important for your children.

As children get into grade school and early junior high they start to question everything (as if you didn't already know that!). They ask ten million "Why?" "How come?" and "Can I?" questions. They even start to question Christianity and the church. There's nothing wrong with this — it's perfectly normal (even if it does drive you up the wall). It's how they learn, start to understand things and begin making choices for themselves.

Sometime during these years children will often want to give their life to Christ. Sometimes they don't have the information they need to make a decision, and many times they aren't even sure what questions to ask. At the same time, you want them to make a decision but are concerned: "Are they old enough?" "If I bring it up, am I pushing them into it?"

My desire for this workbook is to help you confront this dilemma in several ways: 1) help give your children the knowledge necessary to make a personal decision for Christ; 2) give them an opportunity to think about this decision, discuss it at home, and make a commitment that will last; and 3) help put your mind at ease that they do know what decision they are making and why.

In His Name,
Doug Gibson

Dear young people,

As you get into grade school and early junior high you have the opportunity to start making some serious decisions for yourself—decisions that will have an impact on the rest of your life. One of the most important of these decisions is whether God and Jesus are going to be a part of your life or not. Many of you have grown up in a Christian home, but have you made a personal decision to follow Christ?

When faced with a question like that, we often have questions of our own— questions like: "What does it mean to be a Christian?" "How do I become one?" "What does God expect of me?" and many others.

This workbook is designed to answer some of your questions. As you grow in your walk with God, you will discover that you keep learning about Christianity all of your life. But for that to happen you must start somewhere, and that somewhere is with a personal decision to follow Christ.

My desire for this workbook is to: 1) help give you the knowledge necessary to make a personal decision for Christ; 2) give you an opportunity to think about this decision, discuss it at home, and make a commitment that will last; and 3) help put your parents' minds at ease that you do know what decision you are making and why.

Doug

WHO IS JESUS?" AND "WHAT IS SIN?"

How would you describe a Christian?

_____

_____

_____

_____

_____

_____

_____

_____

_____

A Christian will do many different things, but to be a **Christian** means: **to be Christlike, or to follow the teachings of Jesus Christ.**

If you wanted to be a professional football player, an actor or a musician you would imitate those kinds of people. You might try to talk like them, dress like them, or act like them. If we are to be like Jesus, it would be helpful for us to learn more about Him.

Where would you look to find out more about Jesus?

_____

That's right; the Bible tells us all about Jesus. It tells us who He is, why He came, and what He did. It also tells us how we can follow Jesus and become Christians.

We're going to start off our study on how to become a Christian by looking at who Jesus is and what He saves us from.

On the next page you will find a crossword puzzle that will help you to find out what the Bible tells us about Jesus.

WHO IS THIS JESUS ANYWAY?

Look up the following verses and fill in the blanks. Find the words that describe Jesus and fit into the crossword puzzle.

DOWN:

1. John 6:35 "Then Jesus declared, 'I am the bread of _____ . He who comes to me will never go hungry, and he who believes in me will never be thirsty.'"

2. Matt 1:23 "The virgin will be with child and give birth to a son, and they will call him _____ — which means 'God with us.'"

3. Matt 3:17 "And a voice from heaven said 'This is my _____, whom I love; with him I am well pleased.'"

6. Luke 4:18 "The Spirit of the Lord is on me, because he has _____ me to preach the good news to the poor" (this fulfills an Old Testament prophecy).

8. Colossians 1:16 "For by him all things were _____: things in heaven and on earth . . ."

9. John 13:13 "You call me _____ and 'Lord,' and rightly so, for that is what I am."

ACROSS

4. Revelation 19:16 "On his robe and on his thigh he has this name written: _____ OF KINGS AND LORD OF LORDS."

5. John 4:42 "They said to the woman: 'We no longer believe just because of what you said; now we have heard for ourselves, and we know that this man is really the _____ of the world.'"

7. John 4:25-26 "The woman said, 'I know that the _____' (called Christ) 'is coming. When he comes, he will explain everything to us'. Then Jesus declared, 'I who speak to you am he.'"

10. Ephesians 2:20 "You are . . . members of God's household, built on the foundation of the apostles and prophets, with Christ Jesus as the chief _____.'"

11. John 14:6 "I am the _____ and the truth and the life. No one comes to the Father except through me."

12. John 15:5 "I am the _____; you are the branches. If a man remains in me and I in him, he will bear much fruit, apart from me you can do nothing."

13. John 1:14 "The _____ became flesh and made his dwelling among us. We have seen his glory, the glory of the One and Only, who came from the Father. . . ."

MATCH-UP

Congratulations! You've just discovered some of the words used to describe Jesus. Do you know what they mean? In this activity match the words describing Jesus with their meanings by drawing a line to connect them.

Son of God

Anointed One

Bread of Life

Son of David

Emmanuel

Messiah

Cornerstone

The Vine

The Way

Savior

King of Kings

Someone who rescues us from danger or from dying.

Means "God with us."

The only path that allows us to come before God is through Jesus.

Jesus is the "top dog"; He sits at the right hand of God and is greater than all others, no matter what their "title" is.

Jesus' Father is God.

Jesus gives us everything that we need. Without Him we would die, but through Him we produce fruit in our lives.

Another word for Christ or Savior. This is a word the Jews would use when they were looking for the Promised One from God.

Another term for Christ. Jesus was specifically chosen and dedicated for a job. He was set apart from the beginning of time by God to die for us. This term has a picture of pouring oil over someone to dedicate them for a certain job.

Jesus was a descendant of David. He was the chosen descendant who had been promised to come and be a blessing to all the nations of the world.

Jesus gives us everything that we need to live; without Him we would die.

Jesus is the basis upon which we build our lives. This term refers to the most important part of a building. The building would fall apart without it.

The Bible also tells us about some of the things that Jesus did while He was living here on earth. What do the following verses tell us about Jesus?

WHAT DID HE DO?

Luke 2:52 _____

_____

_____

Mark 1:13 _____

_____

_____

_____

Luke 4:15 _____

_____

_____

Luke 7:21 _____

_____

Luke 7:12-15 _____

_____

Matthew 8:24-26 _____

_____

Luke 23:32-34 and 44-47 _____

_____

_____

Matthew 28:5-6 _____

_____

HOW DID JESUS FEEL?

Mark 10:21 _____

_____

John11:5 _____

_____

Mark 3:5 _____

_____

Luke 10:21 _____

_____

Matthew 14:14 _____

_____

John 11:32-35 (especially 35) _____

_____

Jesus was called by a lot of names and did a lot of things while He was alive here on earth. Most of these descriptions fall into three categories:

1. The divine (Godlike) nature of Christ. What names and descriptions have you found that fit this?

_____

_____

_____

2. Jesus' life here on earth. Jesus had many of the same experiences, temptations and feelings that you have. What names and descriptions have you found that fit here?

_____

_____

_____

3. The purpose of Jesus' coming to earth, living, and dying for us. What things have you found that fit here?

_____

_____

You should have found the word **savior** to fit in this third group.

If you were in a burning building and a fireman came and rescued you, we would say that he saved you from the fire. You could call him your **savior** because he had saved your life from the fire that was going to kill you.

If we are going to call Jesus our **Savior**, then we need to know what He's saving us from and why we need to be saved in the first place.

Jesus saves us from our SINS.

What are some sins that people commit? If you need help, look up Exodus 20:1-17 or Galatians 5:19-21 for a couple of lists of sins. _____

_____

The Bible clearly tells us what God wants us to do; it also tells us that if we do the things God doesn't want us to do or if we don't do what He asks us to do, then we are sinning. The real definition of sin is to disobey God.

This can be anything from lying, stealing, or cheating, to simply disobeying our parents when they give us chores to do or tell us to go to bed.

Obviously we've all blown it. In fact, Romans 3:23 tells us: "All people have sinned and are not good enough for God's glory" (ICB). You may have lived a pretty good life, but if you've blown it even once (and we all have), then you are a sinner and in need of a **Savior**. Being a sinner comes with a very stiff penalty, and once we've sinned there is nothing we can do to save ourselves.

THE MONKEY TRAP

In Africa, many tribesmen have a very simple way of trapping monkeys. They will hollow out a coconut and cut a small hole just big enough for a monkey's hand to fit into the coconut. A tribesman will walk up to the trees where the monkeys live and tie the coconut to a stake. He will take a shiny object or a piece of candy and hold it up for the monkeys to see, and then he will slowly place the object into the coconut. After the tribesman leaves, a monkey will come down out of the trees and stick his hand into the coconut and grab the candy. The only problem is that when he makes a fist inside the coconut, he can't pull his hand back out. The monkey wants the object so much that he won't let go. The tribesman simply walks back and puts him in a cage. Some monkeys have been known to starve to death rather than let go of the bait.

How is the monkey trap like sin? _____

_____

ACTIVE OPTION: THE MONKEY TRAP

If you want to experience the monkey trap, you can take a one-gallon empty plastic jug and cut a hole in the side of it. Make the hole just large enough for a baseball to fit snugly inside. Take a piece of rope and tie it to a doorknob; tie the other end to the handle of the jug. Place the baseball inside the jug and then put your hand in the jug and try to remove it without letting go of the baseball. If the hole that you cut is small enough, you won't be able to do it without letting go of the ball (or tearing up the plastic jug) Remember that the coconut shells are much stronger than plastic jugs. How does it feel to be caught in a trap from which you could be free if you would only let go of the ball? We would feel kind of dumb if we got caught in that kind of a trap, but we do it all the time with sin. Satan gets us to sin by making it look like something that we want.

Materials

One Gallon
Plastic Jug

Cut hole on side
of jug the size of
a baseball.

Take a piece of rope and tie
it to a doorknob; tie the other
end to the handle of the jug.
Place the baseball inside the
jug and then put your hand
in the jug and try to remove
it without letting go of the
baseball.

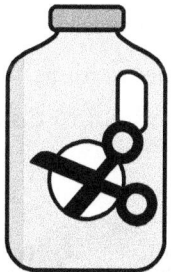

The Bible also describes sin like this: When an archer shoots at a target and misses the bulls-eye, he is missing his mark or target. When we see what God wants us to do but don't do it, we are missing our mark or target, and that is what sin is in our lives.

MISSING THE MARK ACTIVITY:

You will get three "shots" in each round.

Round #1 Place the tip of your pencil on the bow and arrow. Close your eyes and without peeking try to hit the bulls-eye.

Round #2 Place the tip of your pencil on the bow and arrow. Keep your eyes open and, looking at the target, move your pencil as fast as you can across the page and try to hit the bulls-eye.

Round #3 This time keep your eyes open and take your time. Carefully guide your arrow to the bulls-eye.

Which round was the easiest? _____ Why? _____

_____

_____

Which round was the hardest? _____ Why? _____

_____

_____

It's the same with hitting the mark with God. We need to know where the target is in order to hit it. When we carefully keep our eyes on God and what we're supposed to be doing, then it's easier not to disobey God by sinning.

MISSING THE MARK SHEET

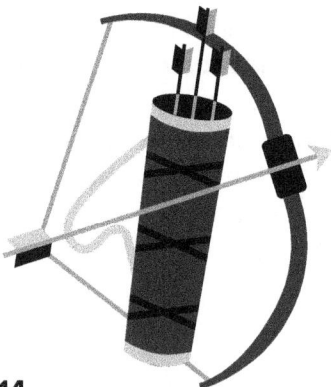

THE FIRST SIN

Read Genesis Chapter 3 and answer the following questions:

What was the first sin? _____

_____

Who committed it? _____

Where did it take place? _____

What was the punishment for each person involved?

The serpent: _____

_____

Eve: _____

_____

Adam: _____

_____

What punishments did Adam and Eve receive together?

_____

_____

Sin had direct consequences for Adam and Eve. It also has a direct impact on our lives today. What are some of the consequences that you face for the sins that you commit?

_____

_____

But these are not the only consequences of our sin. The greatest consequence of sin is the one that we face at the end of our lives. Hebrews 9:27 says "Everyone must die once. After a person dies, he is judged" (ICB).

The greatest penalty that Adam and Eve received was that they were no longer able to walk in the Garden with God. They had separated themselves from God because of their disobedience. When we stand before God on the judgment day, our sins will separate us from God as well.

What do we call the place that God will send those who are separated from Him?

_____

PICTURES OF HELL

The following verses describe what our punishment in Hell will be like. After you've read them, draw a picture in the space provided of what you think Hell might look like. Be ready to explain what the different parts of your picture mean. Matthew 5:22; Luke 16:23; Revelation 20:10; Matthew 22:13; Matthew 25:30; Matthew 25:46

Do you think that God wants to punish us?

_____

God punishes disobedience because He is just and fair. You and I both know that when we do something wrong we deserve to be punished. That's only fair, and God is fair.

How many rules did Adam and Eve have in the Garden?

_____

If God hadn't put the tree in the garden, would Adam and Eve ever have sinned?

_____

God put the tree in the garden because he wanted Adam and Eve to choose to obey and follow him. He didn't want them to be forced to obey.

ACTIVE OPTION: RECORDED COMPLIMENTS

Think of it this way. Get a smartphone and open the voice recording app. Now, tap the record button, and spend the next 2 minutes telling yourself what a great person you are. Tell yourself how beautiful, funny, and smart you are over and over. Talk about your great hair and stylish clothes, your athletic and musical abilities. Now, stop recording, tap "Play," and listen to what a great person you are.

How does it feel to hear all those compliments you just heard about yourself?

_____

_____

Did they really mean anything? _____

_____

No, they didn't mean anything because the recording app had no choice but to say those things about you. Now if your best friend had willingly said those things about you, then they would have meant something.

That's why God put the tree in the Garden — so that Adam and Eve could choose to obey and love Him. If they chose to love Him, then it would have meaning.

Ever since Adam and Eve lost that relationship of walking in the Garden with God, people have been trying to get it back. Sin cut us off from God, but what could we do about it?

THE OLD TESTAMENT LAW:

There are a couple of lessons that God taught throughout the Old Testament that we need to focus on for just a minute or two.

God, in effect, said in the Old Testament, "OK, you want to be perfect, then you must follow these commandments." He gave his people the 10 commandments and several dozen others as well. If we could obey all of these laws, then He would let us into heaven.

Think about this: Adam and Eve couldn't obey one rule all of the time. How in the world could anyone obey all of the laws of the Old Testament? The answer is easy. They couldn't, and God knew that. He wanted to teach us that we couldn't do it alone. He wanted us to cry out for a Savior.

Fill in the rhyming blanks on the tombstones below of those who tried to make it to heaven their own way.

Mary Drake is down with the rest; She thought she'd get to heaven by doing her _____.

Here lies Bobby Brooks. He tried to get to heaven on his good _____.

This is the grave of Sam Bunny. He thought the trick was to buy his way with _____.

Down below is Sally Mends; Thought she'd get to heaven if she had lots of _____.

Joe Cool has gone too far; Tried to get to heaven in his brand new _____.

King George had a crown on his _____; But where did that get him now that he's dead?

The second lesson that we need to look at is the lesson taught through the animal sacrifices in the Old Testament. God told His people to come to His temple and to kill and then burn in sacrifice the finest animals in their flocks. They would look for the best animals they could find, the ones with no birth defects, diseases, or wounds. Then they would take this innocent creature that had done nothing wrong and sacrifice it to God. When they did this, God would allow the blood of the animal to act as a covering for their sins. The blood of animals couldn't take away their sin, but God allowed it to cover their sins until Jesus came and took them away.

God instructed them to do this because He was teaching them a lesson about the coming Savior. They needed to know that the price for sin was death. They needed to know that only a pure and blameless (sinless) sacrifice could cover their sins. He was teaching them that this was what the coming Savior would have to do.

Look up John 3:16 and write it here:

_____

_____

God is fair, and in all fairness we should have to pay the price for our punishment. Because God loves us, He has said that even though sin must be punished, someone who is sinless may die in place of the sinner.

Civil War Story

In the American Civil War the North had all men of a certain age sign up for the draft. If your name was chosen, you were required to go fight in the war. The North didn't care who showed up just as long as the right number of soldiers were ready for battle. If 10,000 men were drafted, then 10,000 men had to show up. Many of the men who were drafted had families that they needed to take care of, so the North allowed someone else to take a person's place. But the person replacing the drafted man couldn't have already been drafted himself. If he had been drafted, he had to be there for himself. If someone had not been drafted, then he could go to war in another person's place.

God has allowed the same thing to happen with us. If someone who has lived a sinless life volunteers to take my punishment on my behalf, God will allow that to happen. God is fair, and in all fairness disobedience has to be punished; but He is also loving, so in love He will allow another to pay the price. We call that person our Savior, and His name is Jesus Christ. He is the Son of God. No one but God could live a sinless life and be able to take our punishment.

Hebrews 9:27 tells us about how we would all be judged after death. But the verses around it give us hope. Hebrews 9:26-28 says; ". . . Christ came only once and for all time. He came at just the right time to take away all sin by sacrificing himself. Everyone must die once. After a person dies, he is judged. So Christ was offered as a sacrifice one time to take away the sins of many people. And he will come a second time, but not to offer himself for sin. He will come again to bring salvation to those who are waiting for Him" (ICB).

JESUS PAID THE PRICE

Jesus came and lived a perfect life here on earth. He never sinned even once, but He took the sins of the entire world on Him when He died.

Let's take a look at the price Jesus paid when He died:

1. When Jesus was arrested, His friends ran away and hid. His friend Judas betrayed Him, and His friend Peter denied Him three times.
2. Before the Sanhedrin (Jewish religious leaders) people lied about Jesus.

3. The Sanhedrin guards spit in Jesus' face. Then they blindfolded Him, slapped Him, and hit Him in the face saying "Tell us who hit you, prophet."

4. Other guards put a purple robe on Him and placed a crown of thorns (2-3 inch long thorns) on His head. They bowed before Him and laughed at Him. Then they took long poles of wood and beat Him with them. They beat Him over the head and drove the thorns into His skull.

5. Pilate had Jesus flogged before He was crucified. A flogging involved being beaten with a whip that was made up of several leather strips. The strips of leather often had pieces of metal, glass and rock attached to the ends of them. Jesus may have been struck as many as 39 times with this whip.

6. Then Jesus was crucified on the cross — one of the most painful ways possible to die.

Jesus suffered all of this, not because He deserved any of it, but because He loved us.

Because we have sinned, we are all separated from God. There is nothing that we can do to deserve to be with God. But out of His love for us, He has allowed His Son to die in our place, so that now we can be with God again.

A good picture of this is illustrated below. Think of God being on one side of a steep valley and us on the other side. Sin is what separates us from God. We have no way of getting across.

God built a bridge through the sacrifice of His Son, so that now we can be with God again.

Connect the dots below to show the bridge that God has made.

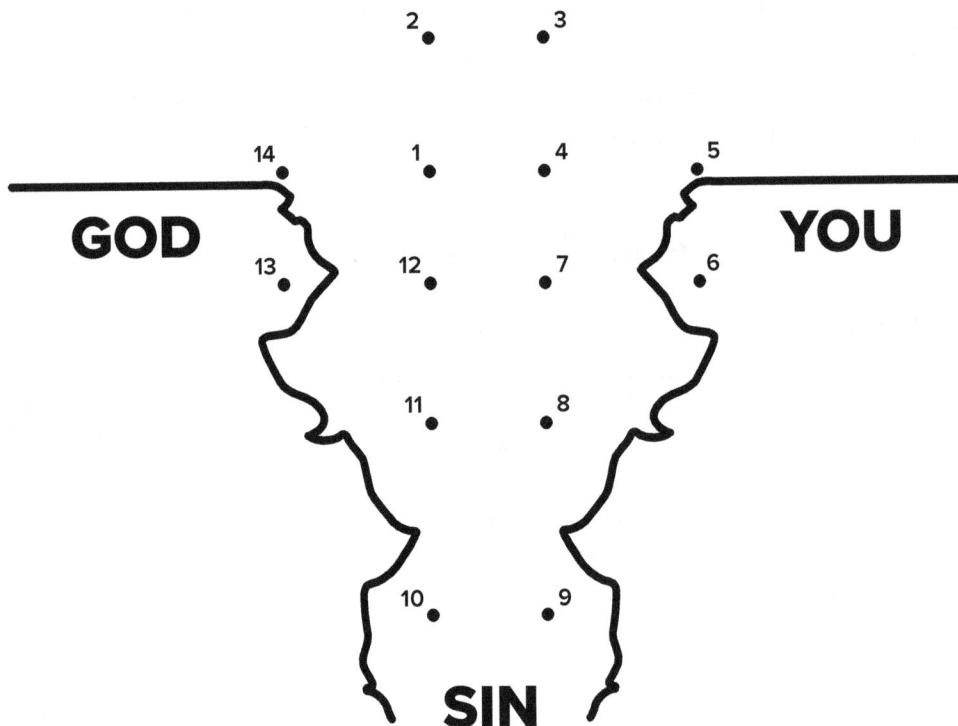

WHAT MUST I DO TO BECOME A CHRISTIAN?

Up to this point this book has been showing us what God is saving us from. It has also shown us that God has done all of the work in taking away our sins. Now we get to the question of what we must do.

God has made it very easy to become a Christian. He has done this because He wants everyone to know that He has saved us. He doesn't want us to brag about what we have done to deserve it, because we can't do anything to deserve it. Salvation is a gift from God.

The Bible shows us the five basic steps in becoming a Christian.

STEP #1 — HEARING: How can you be a follower of Christ if you've never heard of Him? Well, of course, you couldn't. So the first step is hearing about Jesus.

What does Romans 10:17 say? _____

_____

_____

_____

What does Romans 10:14 say? _____

_____

_____

_____

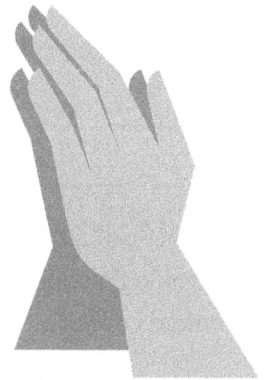

STEP #2 — BELIEVING/FAITH: After you hear about Jesus, you can either believe that it is true or not. You either believe that Jesus is the Son of God and our Savior or you don't. If you believe, we call that having *faith*.

Who does John 20:21 say sent Jesus? _____

_____

_____

What does Romans 3:22 say? _____

_____

What does Mark 16:16 say? _____

_____

What does Acts 16:30-31 say? _____

_____

STEP #3 — REPENTING: Repent means to "about face" or turn around. When we repent, we quit doing what we want to do and instead start doing what God wants us to do. Repenting also involves being sorry for our past actions and seeking forgiveness for them.

What does Acts 2:38 say? _____

_____

_____

What does Jesus say in Luke 13:5? _____

_____

_____

What does Luke 15:10 say? _____

_____

_____

STEP #4 — CONFESSING: Confessing means to say something. You can confess good things (like when you tell people that you believe in Jesus), and you can confess mistakes that you've made (like when a criminal confesses to the judge that he committed a crime).

Repentance naturally leads us to want to confess our mistakes to God, so that He will forgive us. Forgiveness of our sins makes us naturally want to confess the Good News that Jesus is Lord of our life.

What does Romans 10:9-10 say? _____

_____

_____

What does 1 John 1:9 say? _____

_____

_____

STEP #5 BEING BAPTIZED: The final step in becoming a Christian is to be baptized.

What does Acts 2:38 say? _____

_____

_____

What does Acts 16:33 say? _____

_____

_____

Jesus commanded us to be baptized when He told the disciples in Matt 28:19, "So go and make followers of all people in the world; baptize them in the name of the Father, the Son, and the Holy Spirit" (ICB).

Baptism has a couple of mental pictures associated with it to help us understand what God has done for us.

Romans 6:4 talks about being buried with Christ in baptism. This helps us to see that our old sinful way of life is put to death when we are baptized. When we become a Christian, we start living a new life for Christ.

Titus 3:4-5 talks about God washing us. We've all been filthy before and needed a good bath. Well, in God's eyes, when we are sinners, we need a good bath. The blood of Christ is what takes away our sins, but the water of baptism reminds us of the cleansing power of God's love.

To see if you understand the steps in becoming a Christian, match the words to the meanings in the following activity.

WHAT DOES IT MEAN?

Hearing	To be bought again. God created us and then Jesus paid the price for our sins.
Faith	To tell others that Jesus is Lord
Repentance	Our old life is buried with Christ, and a new life begins
Confession	When our ears first discover Jesus
Confession	A bath that reminds us that we are washed clean of our sins through the blood of Jesus
Redeemed	Telling God about the mistakes that we've made and asking for forgiveness
Baptized	Believing that Jesus is the Son of God and our Savior
Baptized	When we "about face" and start following God's directions

IF GOD HAS DONE ALL OF THE WORK, THEN WHY DO I HAVE TO DO THESE THINGS TO BE SAVED?

Do you think that Jesus' sacrifice on the cross could have taken away every sin ever committed? Of course it could.

But if God had done that, then we would have had no choice but to go to Heaven.

Do you remember the tree in the Garden? _____

Why was it there? _____

_____

Do you remember the recording activity that we did? Why didn't any of those compliments on the recording mean anything? _____

_____

_____

God could have allowed the sacrifice of His Son to remove all sins. But He wants you to choose to accept His gift. He wants you to choose to love and obey Him.

Think about Christmas morning. When you wake up, there are lots of presents under the tree with your name on them. You didn't buy them, earn them, or even deserve them. But people who love you have bought them for you. They're free, and they're yours. But you still have to accept them; you have to go open them up and take them. If you didn't, they'd just stay under the tree.

That's the way it is with God. He's got these great gifts for you waiting under the tree, but you have to choose to accept them. You do that by following his Son and becoming a Christian.

Look up the following verses to see what gifts God has in store for you. When you find out what the gift is, write it down in the gift with that verse on it.

GOD'S GIFTS TO YOU

John 3:16   Romans 6:23   Romans 6:4

Acts 2:38   Ephesians 2:8   2 Corinthians 5:1

1 John 3:1   1 John 1:9

JOHN 3:16

EPHESIANS 2:8

1 JOHN 3:1

ROMANS 6:4

1 JOHN 1:9

ACTS 2:38

2 CORINTHIANS 5:1

ROMANS 6:23

One of the greatest gifts that God gives us is the chance to be with Him forever in Heaven. In the next two word searches let's find the things that will be in Heaven with us, and the things that won't be there. Be sure to look for diagonals and words spelled backwards.

THINGS IN HEAVEN

P	R	E	I	C	I	T	Y	A	L	C	B
S	A	C	H	R	I	S	T	I	A	N	S
I	T	S	A	E	F	N	L	I	G	H	T
O	T	O	R	I	F	A	K	J	I	L	H
W	E	N	I	B	I	Y	B	E	O	I	R
L	I	G	O	L	D	A	I	S	C	Y	O
O	V	S	B	N	O	E	N	U	I	S	N
V	I	T	A	N	G	E	L	S	I	R	E
E	T	I	A	C	P	L	N	I	D	L	O
D	U	R	M	P	C	Z	X	A	Q	J	E

FILL IN THE BLANKS FOR SOME HINTS ON WHAT TO LOOK FOR:

For God so ___ ___ ___ ___ ___ the world

Our Savior: ___ ___ ___ ___ ___

God's messengers: ___ ___ ___ ___ ___ ___

Lots of food: ___ ___ ___ ___ ___

God's chair: ___ ___ ___ ___ ___ ___

Jesus' Father: ___ ___ ___

Followers of Christ: ___ ___ ___ ___ ___ ___ ___ ___ ___ ___

Streets of ___ ___ ___ ___

Choir singing ___ ___ ___ ___ ___

Opposite of darkness is ___ ___ ___ ___ ___.

Old is ___ ___ ___

Sadness is ___ ___ ___

THINGS NOT IN HEAVEN

```
L   A   T   B   A   C   R   Y   I   N   G   B
E   F   T   E   G   U   D   T   S   I   N   D
S   E   I   L   O   R   C   O   H   A   I   D
I   A   B   E   R   S   F   V   Y   P   N   S
C   R   D   I   S   E   A   S   E   J   R   N
K   B   A   P   A   E   T   G   C   A   U   O
N   D   E   A   T   H   L   S   E   R   O   L
E   R   V   V   A   A   J   T   R   D   M   V
S   L   I   D   N   T   A   F   A   W   P   O
S   E   L   G   O   E   N   E   C   D   I   H
```

FIND THE FOLLOWING THINGS THAT ARE NOT IN HEAVEN:

Crying, sin, lies, curse, mourning, sickness, disease, satan, evil, hate, tears, pain, death

AFTER I BECOME A CHRISTIAN
WHAT DOES GOD EXPECT OF ME?

Keep in mind that you can't earn the gifts we talked about in Lesson Three; they are freely given by God. But if we are to be His children, then God does have some expectations for our lives.

If you remember, a repentant person was going to change his ways, to stop doing sinful, disobedient activities and to start following God's ways.

Romans 8:13 says "If you use your lives to do the wrong things your sinful self wants, then you will die spiritually. But if you use the Spirit's help to stop doing wrong things you do with your body, then you will have true life" (ICB).

This illustrates two of the things that we need to do as we live our Christian life.

1. We need to read the Bible. How else would we learn to do what God wants us to do?
2. When we find out what God wants us to do (for example, when we read in Exodus about honoring and obeying our parents), then we need to do it.

There are other things that we need to do as well.

We need to pray to God. You can talk with him, confess your sins, ask for help, and ask God to help others.

We need to sing songs and worship God in private and with others.

We need to go to church. We worship together, teach each other, and encourage each other in church.

READ THE BIBLE WORSHIP GOD　　**OBEY THE BIBLE GO TO CHURCH & FELLOWSHIP**　　**PRAY TO GOD MAKE DISCIPLES**

Jesus commanded his disciples to go and make disciples of the whole world. When we become a Christian, we become His disciples and we need to tell others about Jesus.

The next activity helps us to see how we can tell others about Christ.

PARENT AND CHILD ACTIVITY: SHARING OUR FAITH

Preparation: 5 Sets of 18 building blocks. **Each set needs to have the same kinds (but not color) of blocks.** For example each set might contain four 1 × 1 blocks, four 1 × 2 blocks, three 1 × 4 blocks, three 2 × 2 blocks, and four 4 × 2 Blocks.

The parent will need to build some object with four of the sets of blocks (but don't let the kids see your objects ahead of time).

Activity: This is a 4-part exercise:

1. Let your child look at your first model only once and then have her try to instruct someone else how to make it. Listening and watching, that person will try to build a copy of the first object. After they're finished, compare the results to the original.
2. Let someone else look continuously at your second model. Have him try to tell your child how to make it, using only his voice. No pointing, gesturing, or touching of the blocks, etc. After they're finished, compare the results to the original.
3. Let your child look continuously at your third model. This time have her use only her hands to help the other person make it. No talking, no touching the blocks, only hand motions. After they're finished, compare the results to the original.
4. Let your child look continuously at the fourth model. This time your child may talk, use her hands and help any way she wants to until the object has been built. After they're finished, compare the results to the original.

Which was the easiest way to build an accurate model? Why? _____

_____

Which was the most difficult? Why? _____

_____

If we had made a fifth model, where everyone was allowed to look at the model, would it have been any easier than the others? Why? _____

_____

Apply this to our lives with Christ.

If we hardly ever look at Him, what kind of model are we?

_____

_____

If we talk about Him, but our actions don't show it, what kind of model are we?

_____

_____

If we point out godly actions but we don't explain them to others or show them in our lives, how can they come to know Him? _____

_____

If we look to Christ, talk about Him, point with our godly actions and show what it means to be a Christian, how much easier would it be for others to come to know Jesus through us?

_____

_____

_____

BUT I CAN'T LIVE A PERFECT LIFE!

As we look at the things God wants us to do, we also need to understand that God does not expect us to be perfect.

The whole point of Jesus' coming to die for us was that we couldn't be perfect on our own. God knew that you couldn't be perfect before you became a Christian, and He doesn't expect you to be perfect once you become one.

He does expect you to try. God has promised to continue to love and to forgive His children, but they (you) have a responsibility to grow in Christ.

Picture it this way: When you were a baby, you couldn't do very many things. Someone else had to feed you, keep you warm, put clothes on you and even change your diaper. But you have grown and matured to the point that you can do these things. You will continue to grow physically until you're an adult. The same thing happens in your spiritual life. When you become a Christian, you are a baby in Christ and you will need a lot of help and forgiveness; but as you mature, you will learn more for yourself about how to follow Christ, and you will sin less. This maturing will continue throughout your entire life.

No, you don't have to be perfect, but you do have to keep your eyes on the Lord and follow Him to the very best of your ability.

GOD WILL BE WITH YOU

When we looked at the presents that God has waiting for us, did you realize that many of those presents are for you to have right now?

When you become a Christian, God immediately forgives you of your sins. You are no longer guilty before Him.

He sends the Holy Spirit to live within you, to comfort and guide you. You will never be alone again; the Spirit of God is always with you.

We can lift up our prayers to God, knowing that He hears them, as a father hears His children. We become a part of God's family, and Jesus claims us as one of His people.

And the greatest gift is still waiting to be opened. That is when we go to live with God forever in Heaven!

THE CHOICE IS YOURS . . .
WHAT ARE YOU GOING TO DO WITH YOUR LIFE?

God has a great love for you. He has done all of the hard work in making it possible for your sins to be taken away.

But you must still decide whether you will accept God's gift or not. The choice is yours. What are you going to do about it?

NOTES

www.ingramcontent.com/pod-product-compliance
Lightning Source LLC
Chambersburg PA
CBHW081252040426
42452CB00015B/2795